Sonia Shyfrin

Earth and Air

In loving memory of my grandfather Lev Komov,
whose poems have inspired me to write

'In Soviet Russia poetry writes you.'
— Online folklore

CONTENTS

PART II. AIR

PART I. EARTH

The Metropolis

Walk a kilometre, and you won't hear English.

Many strange paths cross here:
princesses and paupers, seekers of happiness.

Some are escaping their motherland.

Some are fighting
or foraging
for it.

In an even stranger way,
the city tangles these paths:
it tore my friends away and united me with an enemy
in a kiss.

This city has taught me to swim in tears and play with
fire. It made me invincible.

THE GREEN LINE

This line with barbed wire fortified,
A wire seen by everyone but me.
This Palestine and Israel of mine,
Two halves that never seem united:

A doll of meat, a candy—oh, whatever,
I can't describe what I myself can't see—
An object, an illusion, a mistake… a woman.

Another half—a friend, a demiurge, a seeker.
Whichever side they find me from, they never

Traverse the line or even see beyond it.

I NEVER KNEW

I never knew
that a kiss,
a passionate kiss of a handsome, rich young man
could upset or disgust me.

Wasn't it all that I've been asking for?
A lonely dream of many nights?

He spoke the language of the soul without knowing it.
His soul was hideous.
He was a prince, but through the onyx dark of his eyes
I saw a monster.

I kissed only a veneer of a prince, I know it.
I felt it when he let me past his skin.

***

I never knew
that a handsome, rich young man, a prince,
could look so miserable
when he understood that his disguise had failed to fool me.

As he walked away,
he was the most dismal sight in the world.

DISCHARM QUARKS

I don't hate you, but deep inside I plea
That in ten to the power of zillion years
When our world approaches the heat death,
Reaching the state of highest entropy,

The photons, leptons, quarks and waves
That once constituted your face
End up in the most distant end from mine
And never touch them in the frozen time.

INTERNATIONAL STUDENTS I

He said she had bad English, because he couldn't understand her.

Me and her,
we understand each other better than anyone in the world,
although my English is worse than his;
For there is a language common to everyone
except the ego.

THEY SAID…

They said, 'He destroyed you'.
Excuse me,
Was his name Creutzfeldt or Jacob[1]?
He destroyed his own soul.
Yours,
He tempered,
Made stronger and wiser.

They said, 'He used you'.
Oh no,
He got used. Before he touched you,
You fucked his *idea*,
Platonically.
You shaped it into art,
Weapons, armour.

You consumed him
To grow, to move a step closer
To your future,
Your truth.

What could he gain?
A split second of pleasure.

---

1 The Creutzfeldt—Jacob disease is an incurable neurodegenerative disorder lethal in 100% cases.

You gained
Momentum, wisdom, experience, power,
Freedom, resilience,
Losing nothing but 80 kg
Of fuckboy meat.

An allegory

Two humans,
we pace in circles in the dark,
tense,
our gazes fixed:
mine on your face, yet wary of the flaming torch you carry,
yours—desperate to catch a glimpse of my moth wings.

I fold them and keep walking as you walk—
in pulsing circles,
beating like a heart.

Stars are my friends,
but they are cold and distant
and indifferent,
whereas your fire is burning here,
inviting.

I shiver. If I fly into the night,
I may not survive it,
but if I burn my wings, I shall dwell on the Earth

and learn to walk
and run
and fight
and dance.

POEMS

They come to me like passion comes to him,
pounce when I walk or sit, or strive for knowledge,
even when I don't want
or can't.
Like a thirsty boy, they stop abruptly on a street
or busy corner
and hold me close and kiss in front of many eyes:
if I resist, like him they lull my reason.

END OF CHILDHOOD

The orange zest of a breakfast muffin
transports me to a bungalow by the sea,
where I savoured it on the terrace,
eight then sixteen,
before heat fell,
observing serene waters
and summits sunburnt.

My head is hazy. A shadow of him
is here:
the slight scent of cologne on my T-shirt.

These images have never overlapped;
What if they merge?

Tomorrow

The tea cup
Burns in my hands.
Tea can't quench the fire under my skin.
So fragrant I can't wait to down it,
It won't cool.

I can't drink champagne;
What if it loosens my tongue?

Tomorrow this time
I won't be in a cosy family home.
I won't be drinking tea

Under his gaze.

INTERNATIONAL STUDENTS II

Two friends boast:

His first snow.
Her first kiss.

'That's not snow!'
'He's not in love.'

'It won't last.'
'Doesn't count.'

One was Russian;
Both were right.

GOLDEN HOUR

I landed into the golden hour.
Emerald hills washed by mellow light,
a soft blanket of moss—the gentle Earth.
The light flooded the airplane, the sun winked
on the edge of the wing,
then on the blue airport glass.

I descend gracefully into the golden hour.

A week since it happened.

A place he cannot reach. He can't reach many—
no,
not because he lacks a Schengen.
His movement is restricted differently.
He cannot travel to universes of different stars,
immortal gardens,
halls of amber with tapestries woven with legends.
Worlds we conjure.

He is stuck not just in a country.

He complained that, if only he had my passport,
he'd go to Europe whenever he felt bored.

But his borders
are harder than any barbed wire,
and his ignorance is deeper than La Manche.

Of what avail are residence permits
when the mind is closed,
when the soul
is isolated by lies?

No one signs a trade deal with a liar.

My passport is inspiration.
My visa is a dare.
My reason for visit is seeking goodness
(sometimes beauty or healing, but always the truth).
My air miles are words (he has about thirty).

They open more gates
than all citizenships combined.

We are born with papers,

but the heart is the one true ID:

other forms were invented
to accommodate those who lacked it.

All borders and bans that he moaned about
are projections of those in the heads
of people like him.

***

Don't picture terrible repercussions befalling them.

You have a kind heart.

Inevitably
you will start pitying them. Pity can grow into sympathy,
and that's what every manipulator desires.

Forgive. Be forgiven. Let go.
Be better.

A UNIVERSAL PRAYER

Fear not death,
for your genes have been there for millions of years
since the scarlet dawn of time,
life's cosmic source.

They'd been there
before pouring into you through your parents;
growing and shapeshifting, transforming and morphing
as stars circled the sky and constellations
changed contours, and they will remain in time's downfall,
the cataract of order, the Second Law,
the arrow
from the tip of which blood ever spills,
the sap of life.

They've been there for millennia
and for millennia they will remain
in different vessels,
perfected and striving for beauty
more Dionysiac than ever.
Even if your line dies out, your particles will not—
trust this
even if you can't trust aught else.
They'll find a way: ash, water, fire, earth, memory.
Ones and zeros,

A's, C's, T's, G's,
they will persist:
a rose, a pouncing cat—or a beast yet unconceived,
a lover's kiss,
a purer, brighter mind.

It all exists because it can exist
and because nothing has destroyed it yet.

OUT

My friend,
you've always hidden your mesmerising wings.
Today
you spread them:
suddenly, late at night, after tea.

I dropped my spoon.

We were astonished, yet
everything made sense.
All pieces fell in place.

Yes, wings—that's how it felt:
a completed image.

All the evil in the world
won't cloud their beauty.

The Blackbird

In the dead of an empty night,
Neither awake nor asleep,
I heard a strange noise.

At first I suspected my flatmates:
It was a Saturday night. The hall
Was like a quarter-moon, half-lit,
An ant-house soaked in alcohol.

Then I realised:
A blackbird warbled,
Its voice painted the dark.

Tinúviël,

A beauty unseen,
A tremulous spark in the cold,
A shoot growing through asphalt.

I opened the curtains and checked:
Dawn was far, my neighbor
Was watching TV across the mews.
The night was alive.
My train departed in several hours.

The blackbird sang—how many times
Did his music enter my dreams?
Maybe I was kept awake
So that I could hear him,
So that I learnt
What secrets the darkness hid
And knew:
I'm never alone in the night.

When else could we talk?

Perhaps he was an envoy of the loving world
Sent to make me sing too;
For I have abandoned my song.
Buried in studies, paper destinies
Longed to unravel.

BEYOND BINARITY

I am yes and no,
One and zero,
The best of both worlds.

I hacked the matrix.

I am an oxymoron,
A contradiction,
A supergirl—

Almost like Virgin Mary.

I am blessed
In a way known but to me
And my siblings in miracles.

In mud I cleanse.
Poison grafts me immunity.

HOMECOMING

I was scared to emerge
From last mesocosm of Britain, the plane.
I observed the change:
From clustered, ordered houses in emerald—
To immense snow fields with scattered decrepit villages.

The cold did not daunt me;

The customs did.

The land of my ancestors.
I walk under their gazes,
I breathe their ash.
But I am torn out of it.
London diffused into me.

But what can erase millennia
From my DNA?

Not the City,
The woods, the ancient skyscrapers.
Pine masts sway
In a boundless sea.
Wind brushes past them and me,
A small child of this place,

A sapling,
A pupil

Of life—always.

Why is the citadel of knowledge
So far from my roots?

I grew up among you.
I'm part of you.
Everything I do there, in a white coat,
Is an extension of my zeal to understand Life
That grew like each of my organs,
Here.

_____(INSERT YOURS)

I fly,
I destroy
Myself,
Crash the plane,
Sink the ship.

But they,

They remain:
Non-material spirit,
A phantom,
A ghost—

If there's no escape,

Then let pain strengthen my heart:
Not break it,
Not harden it.

ANTHROPIC PRINCIPLE?

All the constants
in place to spawn life—hundreds.

My life, as Life itself, is woven
of lucky coincidences—thousands.

Not just physical constants:

a rejection when I gave my all,
an impulse to go when I locked myself up,
a tap on the screen.

What if I turned left, not right?

A precious bond would evanesce.
How many turns did I miss?
I cannot know,
yet I've reached a beautiful place.

CHIVALRY IS NOT DEAD

I am better trained in fighting,
but still, they are my knights.

Their spirits are strong.

Their minds shine—not armours.

Gold lies in their souls—not vaults.

They have—
Not noble blood
but something more precious and rare:
noble hearts.

PART II. AIR

Prologue

Stranger, hearken to the lonely wind.
He's seen lands uncharted
Guarded by river-serpents,

Bathed in milky fogs spilled from mountains,
Listened to songs unheard,
Voyaged over scorching dunes

Where the salt-woven sea
Washes the golden firmament.
A messenger of the clear sky,

He tousled fathomless oceans,
Blue reaches pitted with waves,
And crashed into fiery dawns

Glowing red above the solemn gates.
But never has he traversed the stone line—
To the abysses beyond the last crosses,

Where time plummets like water
And star-paved roads burn out,
Stretching above a void without end.

There, on the last threshold, voyagers
Cast their final looks upon the world
Before stepping into the unknown.

The City of Ruby

The mountains clad in evening lazurite,
The logs of sunset smouldering and smoking,
And crowned with golden turrets, stands alight
The flaming City of Ruby.

The deadly frost's returned to reign
Over the halls of silent deserts,
But in the sand-heart, night and day,
The Ruby City burns, unfading.

The chilling winds in distance drone
Upon the fields of terracotta,
Yet in the rubies smoulder on
The chars of the sun's only stronghold,

Where glimmer eerie scarlet dreams;
The phantoms of a lifeless valley.
For not a spark of love ignites—
Warm blood sustains alight the rubies.

SURVIVOR

The silent seas
In hoar bound,
Smouldering East
With ashes crowned.
Beyond the frost
A feeble light;
All pain is lost
In endless white.
A frozen gaze
Through paleness cast,
Insipid waves
Sharper than glass.

Yet ever burns
The inner call;
More firm than words
Compels to haul
Through ocean tides,
Through tears ice-bound,
Too weak to fly,
Too weak to drown.
My heart in flames—
A throbbing dawn.
Through frozen planes
I carry on.

I WANT TO BE THERE

I read about fiery heavens
And sunsets like seraphim blades,
Horizons with wrath incandescent
By eagle-like clouds overloomed,
Air smoky and pregnant with menace.

I read and I want to be there.

I read about thunder and tempests —
Storms smiting the shape of the Earth
And tearing the old world asunder.
Waves towering, tossing and throwing
Lost souls with no lighthouse or sign

To guide them. I want to be there.

I read about moments of silence—
Great silence that deafens the world,
For millions of flowers on water—
A handful of souls in exile.
All powers and elements humbled;

I grieve and I want to be there.

I read about hope everlasting,
Defying oppression and death,

Last smouldering embers igniting
A star that is brighter than day,
Reborn from the dust and the ashes.

I want to be part of this hope.

And, threaded through each word and letter,
Is love that I seek in the book.
All distance and time overthrowing,
Reshaping the world with a touch
In many ungraspable guises.

This love I desire to become.

MARCH

Old
Cross,
Woods
Quiet.
Face –
Young,
March –
White.

Step,
Crack.
Hush—
Glimpse:
Glade
Still.
Blade –
Swift.

"Friend,
How?"
Thoughts
Hurt.

Black
Soul,
Gaze –
Cold.

Steel
Rings,
Swords
Gleam—
Lunge,
Moan.
Breath –
Steam.

Fell
Down;
Cry
Ceased.
Red
Snow,
White
Face.

Torn
Cape,
Hard
Stone.
Veiled
Grief;

Proud
Scorn.

POIGNANT MOMENTS

Parting with transiently made friends,
Discussing unrequited feelings with someone who's known them,

A children's choir singing Christmas carols,
When plans that kept you going fail,

When a couple that seemed to be forever breaks up,
When your rival cries on your shoulder.

'Devoted to the Moon'

> '...Isildur said no
> word, but went out by night and did a deed for
> which he was afterwards renowned. For he passed alone
> in disguise to Armenelos and to the courts of
> the King, which were now forbidden to the Faithful;
> and he came to the place of the Tree...'
>
> — J. R.R. Tolkien, *The
> Silmarillion*

Of silhouettes of broken nights

I wove my cloak. Horizons burning
Crowned with a wreath of scorching steel,
The sun ascends—a flaring wheel
Grinding the edges of the morning.

Of echoes of tormented cries

I forged my sword, and calling out
To grinning heavens for protection,
Among the wavering reflections
Alone I venture for the light.

I am a mortal with a shield

Of the sun disc's unyielding shadow.
I'm ashes, kindled by a spark
Of thousand agonies on fire.
The world pulsating in my eyes,
But my resolve will never falter,
Death looms, a firmament of dark—

I clench the fruit of Ninquëlotë.

In labyrinths of temple fires
The sunset rays are only sacred.
The price we pay for our sins—
The chilling cold of Western winds,
Our hopes to dust reduced and wasted.

I am alive, but time flows by;
My blade is rinsed, but not in water.
Farewell, Land of the fallen Star, Farewell—

Let memories of days of fire
Glare in the night—a crimson diamond.
The flames will not dance on the white
And holy heart of Atalantë.

THE DUEL

I

Thou art ice daring to challenge sacred fire, a mortal bearing metal
in his eyes. Heavens and earth shall never compromise, and thy
day's ephemeral like a flash of emerald where firmaments impale the
ocean. Sunset's thy fate, sunset thy ragged banner. So face thy death
in full sail, and behold—like ash the last light of the day precipitates
beyond the fog, thine agony and my supreme delight.

Thou sayest, the Powers blessed thee? Nonsense: thy star can't break
its fall.

The path has but two ends: an altar radiant or the sea's coldest
deep, a flaming halo on your brow or frost. Two ends, yet only
one decisive turn. Your world's ablaze, its rotten morals writhe on
scorching coal; the crucible of My discord shall melt the steel of thy
weary gaze.

Thou sayest, truth is power? Lies. All truths are but reflection of
the one: there'll be no second master of the minds. The sentence's
absolute and sealed with gore:

in flames or on the ocean's darkest floor,

just one will live to see the break of dawn.

II

Thou spoke the truth: my strife is doomed.

I may win every battle but cannot emerge victorious from the war. If not a sword, then age will cut my thread, not your fire but the Lord's will melt the ice and dry the blood in tangled veins.

But death is not the end; it is a change.

Thou spoke the truth: the path has but two ends, but only mine. Thou can't deceive thyself with sycophantic words, nor steer away from the predestined road—a lifetime bright and long, but not eternal.

Time's on thy side, but it's Creator is on mine.

I'll die; so will my son, then his. The waves of Lethe may erase my blood but not the memory of retribution.

Thy fate belongs to thee as much as sun rays to the moon.

Thou spoke the truth: my strife is doomed,

but it's not vain.

***

Forgive me; fate is hard to come to terms with,
Although I know that you are not to blame
For me hallucinating stellar landscapes
Where you see only walls sterile and plain.

However, pride is nothing to step over;
I've been there and I know what you may feel.
But is it wrongful to endure in silence
And hide the flame behind an iron seal?

No equals no. Don't touch what isn't yours;
Let light incinerate me from inside,
I promise: I will follow the commandment
Behind your eyes immutably inscribed,

Having no right to tread paths meant for others,
Having no power to avert my gaze.

OF LOVE, REVENGE AND GREEK CUISINE

A saganaki hisses on the stove;
Like me in your embrace, it melts and oozes.
Tonight your dreams shall not come true, my love:
Cheese warms my soul and body rather better.

You ask me, sweetheart, why my voice as chill
As cubes of feta in a salad dressing?
You speak your love, and yet when darkness falls
Eat every piece yourself without confessing.

Above the sea the dawn is blushing red;
Like fried halloumi on a grill, it glistens.
You beg me for a treat, but all in vain:
Revenge and cheese are sweeter than your kisses.

FROST PATTERNS

Fell silence on the blueness of the winter;
Like frost, it rests upon the humming wires.
Amidst the snowy haze towns gleam and smoulder,
And rains of tears are bound in crystal ice.

The glass blends whirls of sparkling reflections
Of Kremlin stars and Christmas fairy lights,
The minus of the eyes in it united
With the omniscient vision of the heart.

I raise a glass of mulled wine to the evening
So that your window also be adorned
With frozen heartbeat by the wordless Spirit,
The One that silent rests beyond the stars.

I WANT TO BECOME A SEA WAVE

If I could choose
What to become for a short time
My answer would be,
Let me turn into a sea wave.
Alone I will cross the world In a waking dream,
And nothing will be able stop me But the wind.
A gull shall find repose on my crest,
Fish shall swim right through me.
I shall deliver catch to the fisherman,
Stingers to the deep,
Those drowning in shipwrecks
To the shore.
I will caress my beloved one,
Water splashing by his feet,
And kill another,
Drag them into the abyss,
And bury in the sea bottom
Those who'll have renounced life themselves.
When wrath wells up in me,
I shall turn to the shore,
Swollen with brine, rise up to the clouds
And collapse on the sinful city,
Wipe it from the Earth's face.

One day at sundown
Sadness will overcome me—
A longing to shatter against the rocks
And be reborn with the first glimpse of morning
In the remote heart of the ocean,
Where human lies
Won't cloud my vision.

Acknowledgements

I am grateful beyond expression to my entire family for their support, to my brother and grandparents for unwittingly nudging me to start writing poetry, to mum for being the first reader of everything I wrote, and an infinitely kind and understanding person, to dad for being the best life coach and an inspiration, and to my Music and History of Arts school teacher, M.G. Gorbenko, for the priceless knowledge and guidance she provided me with.

Lightning Source UK Ltd.
Milton Keynes UK
UKHW040457020720
365831UK00007B/230